PROVINCETOWN
DISCOVERED

PROVINCETOWN
DISCOVERED

4·23·86

Dear Mom,
Here's a little
picture book of
my town. When-
ever you need to
Relax just open
it up and imagine
yourself in
Cape Cod —
Love,
Bruce

THE FISHING VILLAGE

WHERE THE PILGRIMS FIRST LANDED

A CAMERA IMPRESSION BY EDMUND V. GILLON JR.

Schiffer Publishing Ltd

Printed in the United States of America.
ISBN: 0-88740-061-2
Published by Schiffer Publishing, Ltd.
1469 Morstein Road, West Chester, Pennsylvania 19380

This book may be purchased from the publisher.
Please include $1.50 postage.
Try your bookstore first.

Front cover: Nighttime illumination of Pilgrim Monument.

Aerial view of Provincetown, photographed by Richard Kelsey of Chatham,
Massachusetts.

Following page: View of Commercial Street framed by a rotting pier.

Title page: House in the West End.

View in the Village of Provincetown.

Woodcut of Commercial Street in the 1830's.

Dedication

To Fred and Doris Sibley with whom I had the pleasure of sharing so many New England excursions.

Foreword

"Provincetown is like an onion. There is here
layer on layer, whorl on whorl. Three civilizations
have met here and formed a unique strain. The
old New Englanders, the Portuguese, and the
summer folk have made a town individual in the
world."

Mary Heaton Vorse
Time and the Town
1942

Provincetown, Massachusetts is a lands-end place. Located
thirty miles out in the Gulf Stream of the Atlantic Ocean, this
small fishing village hugs the narrow bayside tip of Cape Cod, a
flexed-arm shaped peninsula. The town is sheltered from the
turbulent sea by a wall of lofty sand dunes that line the ocean
side. Provincetown's unique and isolated setting is dramatically
revealed upon entering the town from the heights of neigh-
boring Truro.

The road from Truro to Provincetown crosses a natural
causeway washed on one side by the waters of Cape Cod Bay,
and bordered on the other by the stillness of a fresh water pond.
This pond nestles at the foot of a mountainous sand dune which
stands, sentinel-like, at the entrance to the town. Beyond the
dune, at a fork in the road, lies the entrance to Commercial
Street, the town's main artery; the thoroughfare that embodies
Provincetown's beguiling character.

Commercial Street is but a narrow lane, originally a pedes-
trian path, which meanders along the shore's edge for a couple
of miles. Its small shops and quaint, wooden houses stand
cheek by jowl along the street, thus evoking images of Medieval
Europe. The Town Hall Park, with its World War I Memorial
monument, is also Commercial Street's Municipal Plaza, a most
delightful place to sit and watch the passing parade. On a lively

Opposite: The town cemetery with the pilgrim monument in the background.

summer evening, such a parade is indeed a very colorful one, a kind of Disneyland version of Times Square by the sea. If the crew members of the whaling ships that once sailed from this small port, could magically return on such an evening, might they not think they had landed in one of the exotic foreign ports they were used to visiting on their world cruises?

Well, today, the world has arrived in Provincetown!

The first world traveler who came to these shores was a Scandinavian explorer, Leif Ericson, who sailed from his homeland to the New England coast, back in 1003. Shortly thereafter, a viking from Iceland, Thorwald, hauled his vessel ashore in order to repair a broken keel. Later, in what is now known as Boston Bay, he was wounded in a skirmish with the local Indians. Sensing his demise, Thorwald requested he be buried at the same spot where his ship had been repaired. He also instructed that his body be buried with a cross at the head and foot of his grave, and that the place be named The Cape of Crosses. More recently, in 1602, Bartholemew Gosnold, an Englishman, arrived on the ship Sparrow Hawk. Anchoring offshore, a great store of codfish was taken. To mark his good fortune, a Gosnold chronicler named the place Cape Cod.

The arrival of the next visitors to what is now Provincetown was an accidental one. The pilgrims, aboard the Mayflower, were actually headed for Virginia, but a harrowing storm at sea forced them to seek shelter inside the protective hook of Provincetown Harbor, at the time listed on Captain John Smith's map as Milford Haven. Before disembarking there, the men of the Mayflower wrote and signed the Mayflower Compact, a document that fathered the forthcoming Declaration of Independence.

The first pilgrim child to be born in the new land, Peregrine White, was delivered aboard the Mayflower. A descendant of this child lives at 466 Commercial Street.

The pilgrims spent five weeks in Provincetown exploring the surrounding coast in search of a suitable place to establish a permanent settlement. But they failed to find such a place, and so they hoisted anchor and set sail for the less exposed Plymouth Bay on the mainland.

From the time of the pilgrims' departure until the 1680's, Provincetown remained unsettled. Fishing attracted the first

Drawn by J. W. Barber—Engraved by S. E. Brown, Boston.

Woodcut of Provincetown harbor in the 1830's, salt mills line the beach at right.

settlers; mackerel and cod were abundant; whales were so numerous that early settlers hunted them from the shore. A hilltop lookout would sight the mammal and point its direction to men on the beach who were standing by, ready to launch their boats for the attack. After killing them, the whales were towed ashore where oil was extracted by boiling the blubber. Later, the whales shunned the bay's shallow waters and the search for them in more remote areas of the ocean resulted in Provincetown's fleets leaving port for two or three years at a time.

The growth of the fishing industry in Provincetown resulted in the swelling of the town's population—from having a predominantly Yankee population, it changed to a mixture of immigrants, mainly Nova Scotians, Irish and later, during the Civil War, a tide of Portuguese fishermen settled there.

Provincetown reached its peak of prosperity during the later part of the nineteenth century. During this period, the harbor was the scene of great activity when as many as 700 ships are

An early twentieth century postcard depicts a panoramic view of the town and harbor as seen from town hill.

said to have been anchored off its shore. There were 54 long wharfs each of which contained caulkers, sailmakers, barrel-makers, riggers, blockmakers, blacksmiths and shipwrights.

At the time, Provincetown was the richest town per capita in the state of Massachusetts. Its fortune, however, abruptly changed in 1859, when oil was discovered in Pennsylvania. Kerosene replaced whale oil as fuel for lamps and this signaled the demise of the whaling industry in Provincetown.

By the turn of the 20th century, the last major influx of settlers began to arrive. They were mostly artists and writers. The artists were attracted by the extraordinary quality of light they found there, a light provided by the reflection from the surrounding ocean waters and the bay. The uniquely pictu-resque character of Provincetown provided a rich variety of subject matter to paint. An artist colony was founded by Charles Hawthorne and in 1899, he opened the Cape School of Art.

Close ties to the New York art world were established

subsequently, and bohemian Provincetown became an extension of Greenwich Village. The more traditional artists of the earlier period were suddenly overshadowed by the arrival in America of Parisian Left-Bank expatriates forced to emigrate by the German invasion of France. Soon, art associations were organized to discuss such issues as Bolshevism, the role of the artist in a socialist society, the promotion of Cubism, Futurism and other Modernisms in art. A small group of aspiring playwrights were also in residence in Provincetown, where they founded the Provincetown Players in an old wharf building. Eugene O'Neill, among other distinguished writers, was invited to show some of his work, and plays staged in Greenwich Village theaters brought fame to the Players.

Today, the tradition of the arts is carried on by the Provincetown Art Association and Museum, which was established in 1914. Some of the Museum's famous members, past and present, include Raphael Soyer, Chaim Gross, Hans Hoffman, Milton Avery and Robert Motherwell.

Above: An 1870 photograph of the town hall which burned in 1877. The Pilgrim Monument now occupies the site.

Opposite: A vintage photograph of the East End. The skyline is dominated by the graceful spire of the church on Commercial Street, which now houses the Heritage Museum.

By means of captioned photographs, this book hopes to share with the viewer the sense of discovery that inspired the taking of the pictures. For all its surface mood of hurly burly, Provincetown is essentially a place that offers rare tranquility. The many views of majestic dunes, sylvan glens and lonely beaches are overwhelming reminders that calmness and solitude are easily found a stone's throw from the lively pace of the town.

Opposite: View from the great dunes of the province lands national seashore, looking down on a fresh water pond and the causeway connecting Truro to Provincetown with Cape Cod Bay on the horizon.

Above: Provincetown from the national seashore.

Opposite: A shingled summer cottage perched on a dune in Mayflower heights.
Above: Two hikers are silhouetted against the sky in the national seashore.

Opposite: Shops along bayside of Commercial Street in the East End.

Above: A picturesque group of shingled structures face the beach at low tide in the West End.

Above: A Greek revival house on Commercial Street in the West End.
Opposite: A West End Shipyard.

A Commercial Street guest house built in 1870 with an inviting two-story sunfilled bay.

A gambrel-roofed cottage with a commodious porch and corner tower. The tower section of this house is illustrated in Edward Hopper's "The Lee Shore."

Following page: Low tide along the Commercial Street waterfront.

Above: The front yard of a house on Commercial Street filled with lobster traps.
Opposite: A low tide in the harbor reveals a giant rusted anchor trapped in the sand.

Opposite: A board and battan faced Gothic revival house in the West End.

Above: A Greek Revival house in the West End.

Opposite: The Provincetown waterfront at sunset.

Above: An off-season tranquility pervades this view of Commercial Street in the West End.

Opposite: A graceful federal-style fence frames the entranceway of this handsome cottage on Cook Street, built in 1850.

Above: A Greek revival house on Nickerson Street built in 1840. Its facade sports a bay generous window, probably a later addition.

Above: A many-gabled cottage on Caver Street. Its design is an odd combination of Greek revival and Carpenter Gothic elements.

Opposite: A backyard view of the graceful spire of the Universalist Church on Commercial Street.

Opposite: Two strollers near center are dwarfed by the vast space of the dunes.

Above: A West End cottage on Commercial Street built in 1850 has two Greek revival doorways.

Opposite: A former church on Commercial Street which now houses the Heritage Museum. A half-scale model of the fishing schooner Rose Dorothea is under construction in its auditorium.

Above: The Heritage Museum's Tower rises above a jumble of many-angled rooftops.

Opposite: A fishing boat returns to safe haven just before an approaching storm.

Above: The "Figurehead House" on Commercial Street built in 1850. Home of Captain Henry Cook whose family dominated the whaling and fishing wholesale industry during the greater part of the nineteenth century.

Opposite: A glimpse of the bay as seen through a narrow passage between two buildings on Commercial Street.

Above: The "Summer Life" on the back decks of a former artists' studio on Commercial Street.

Opposite: A horse and carriage transport a top-hatted guide and tourist along Commercial Street.

Above left: A former lumber wharf built in 1845 on Commercial Street now houses an antique shop.

Above right: A firehouse turned into a leather shop on Commercial Street.

Opposite: The "Isaac" fishing boat of New Bedford unloading its day's catch at MacMillan Wharf.

Above: Summer rentals on an old wharf in the West End.

A shingle and clapboard cottage on Commercial Street.

Mid-day strollers passing by shops on Commercial Street in the East End.

Opposite: A fish shed on the beach at 227 Commercial Street.

Above: A mansard roofed, Second Empire-styled guest house on Commercial Street being dressed up for the summer season.

Above: A sleeping child and dog in the town cemetery.
Opposite: A sylvan glade in the national seashore.

Opposite: The Atlantic Ocean as seen from the top of a dune in the national seashore.

Above: A fresh water pond covered with lilies in the national seashore.

Following page: The town cemetery with a glimpse of the bay on the horizon.

Opposite: A nature trail in the national seashore.

Above: An elegant stoop and an urn-topped fench grace this house on Cook Street.

Opposite: The Universalist Church on Commercial Street.

Above: A picturesque East End shingled-cottage on Commercial Street.

The quintessential summer inn on Commercial Street with vintage car parked in front yard.

A gambrel roof East End cottage on Commercial Street.

Above: The town hall and police station on Commercial Street, built in 1886.

Opposite: The Pilgrim Monument towering above the roofs of houses on Bradford Street. The tallest granite structure in America which was built to commemorate the first landing of the pilgrims in 1907.

Opposite: A gable-fronted cottage in the West End.

Above: A Second Empire-styled house on Commercial Street.

Opposite: A West End Greek revival house with "lightning splitter" gable.

Above: An overturned gravestone in the town cemetary.

Above: A seaside farm in the East End.
Opposite: An elegant little "Three Quarter Cape" on Baker Street.

Above: A tall-gabled East End house with side entrance.
Opposite: A shady lane in the West End.

Opposite: A beautifully restored Greek revival house in the West End.

Above: A late afternoon sun lights the spire of the Universalist Church on Commercial Street.

Right: The quintessential charm of a Cape Cod cottage is expressed in this West End doorway.

Dead gull on granite breakwater.

Marble dog in town cemetery.

Opposite: The East End as seen from the top of the Pilgrim Monument.

Above: The West End viewed from the Pilgrim Monument.

Above: A hip-roofed captain's house on Commercial Street with front windows shut to protect it from the winter gales.

Opposite: A West End shop facade which suggests a Shaker simplicity.

Above: A hip-roofed, shingled house on Commercial Street with its typical projecting doorway vestibule.

Opposite: The water of the Harbor Marina sparkles under the October sunlight.

Opposite: A mansion on Gosnold Street. Note the eccentric placement of Ionic capitals in the front-entrance portico.

Above: The Provincetown Art Association.

Right: A delightful half-house with a bold Greek revival doorway.

A Second Empire cottage on Center Street built in 1880.

Low tide in the West End.

Following page: A West End wharf.

Above: A dune road in the national seashore.
Opposite: A West End wharf.

Above: A clapboard cottage with shingled addition in the West End.
Opposite: A Greek revival house on Commercial Street in the East End.

Above: A West End cottage with twin bay windows.
Opposite: The oldest house in Provincetown built in 1746.

Opposite: Approaching storm in Mayflower Heights.

Above: Hip roofed, brick end house on Bradford Street which once housed Provincetown's first bank in its front parlor.

Right: A weathered Greek Revival East End cottage.

Opposite: A Great American elm towers over this east East End Street leading down to the bay.

Above: The steep-gabled Caleb Cook house on Bradford Street.

Opposite: A former church on Commercial Street in the West End now transformed into this charming home.

Above: The dunes in the national seashore.

Above left: A perky little cottage in the East End.

Above right: A shingled cottage with second-story overhangs on Commercial Street in the West End.

Opposite: A Second Empire-styled cottage in the East End on Commercial Street.

Opposite: A house in the East End on Commercial Street which possesses a rare asset for that street, it has a generous front lawn.

Above: A marshy West End inlet.

Above: A colorful West End cottage. Note the clay head chimney pot near the top right.

Opposite: The granite breakwater connecting the West End to Long Point.

Above: A fine Greek revival house on Bradford Street.

Opposite: A late afternoon view of Provincetown from Route 6A.

THANKFUL R.
Wife of
Sears Rich...
Died Mar. 31, 1869,
...d 6... Y.. 3 mos.
4 Days.

We know that our loved one
Is happier far in yonder
Glorious home, than aught
We can conceive, and yet, how
Our poor human hearts are
Ever yearning for love that
Was so dear; how selfishly
We cling to her loved memory
As she walked with us in the
Low vale, and see not through
Our tears the golden streets
Where now her footsteps fall.

A broken marble tombstone in the town's cemetary.

A "Three Quarter Cape" cottage undergoing restoration.

Above: Low tide along Commercial Street on the West End.
Opposite: Provincetown from the dunes in the national seashore.

The national seashore dunes.

The sparkling waters of the harbor from a beachside deck.

Opposite: A Carpenter Gothic cottage in the West End.

Above: A Greek revival cottage with horizontal plank fence on Bradford Street in the East End.

Right: One of the Commercial Street's most diminutive shops appropriately called "The Little Store."

Above: A Queen Anne-styled villa on Commercial Street in the West End.
Opposite: The West End shoreline at low tide.

Above: MacMillan wharf and the great break-water of Provincetown's harbor.

Left: The Atlantic House on Masonic Place, a Provincetown institution, built as a hotel in 1812. Its ancient bar dates back to 1798.

Opposite: A giant elm towers over a weathered cottage on Commercial Street in the West End.

A "Three Quarter Cape" cottage in the West End.

A barber chair and three sawed-off bathtubs grace the pebbled yard of this house on Freeman Street.

Above: Shops along the bay side of Commercial Street in the West End.
Left: A two-story veranda on Commercial Street in the West End.
Opposite: Portico of house on Gosnold Street.

Town crier, center, in pilgrim garb greets disembarking passengers at MacMillan Wharf.

Sculpture of sleeping woman on Masonic Lane.

Following page: Wharfs at low tide in the West End.